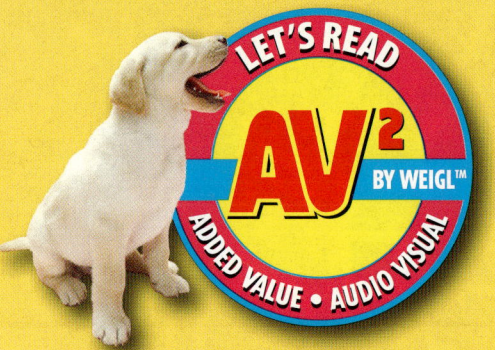

Go to www.av2books.com, and enter this book's unique code.

BOOK CODE

J611318

AV² by Weigl brings you media enhanced books that support active learning.

AV² provides enriched content that supplements and complements this book. Weigl's AV² books strive to create inspired learning and engage young minds in a total learning experience.

Your AV² Media Enhanced books come alive with...

 **Audio**
Listen to sections of the book read aloud.

 **Video**
Watch informative video clips.

 **Embedded Weblinks**
Gain additional information for research.

 **Try This!**
Complete activities and hands-on experiments.

 **Key Words**
Study vocabulary, and complete a matching word activity.

 **Quizzes**
Test your knowledge.

 **Slide Show**
View images and captions, and prepare a presentation.

... and much, much more!

Published by AV² by Weigl
350 5th Avenue, 59th Floor New York, NY 10118
Websites: www.av2books.com   www.weigl.com

Copyright ©2015 AV² by Weigl
All rights reserved. No part of this publication may be reproduced, stored in a retrieval system, or transmitted in any form or by any means, electronic, mechanical, photocopying, recording, or otherwise, without the prior written permission of the publisher.

Library of Congress Control Number: 2014934876

ISBN 978-1-4896-1130-7 (hardcover)
ISBN 978-1-4896-1131-4 (softcover)
ISBN 978-1-4896-1132-1 (single user eBook)
ISBN 978-1-4896-1133-8 (multi-user eBook)

Printed in the United States of America in North Mankato, Minnesota
1 2 3 4 5 6 7 8 9 0 18 17 16 15 14

052014
WEP150314

Project Coordinator: Katie Gillespie   Design and Layout: Ana María Vidal

Weigl acknowledges Getty Images as the primary image supplier for this title.

Let's Celebrate American Holidays
Memorial Day

CONTENTS

2	AV² Book Code
4	When Is Memorial Day?
6	What Is Memorial Day?
8	General John A. Logan
10	Where We Celebrate
12	Coming Together
14	How We Celebrate
16	More Traditions
18	Tomb of the Unknowns
20	Special Celebrations
22	Memorial Day Facts
24	Key Words/

Log on to www.av2books.com

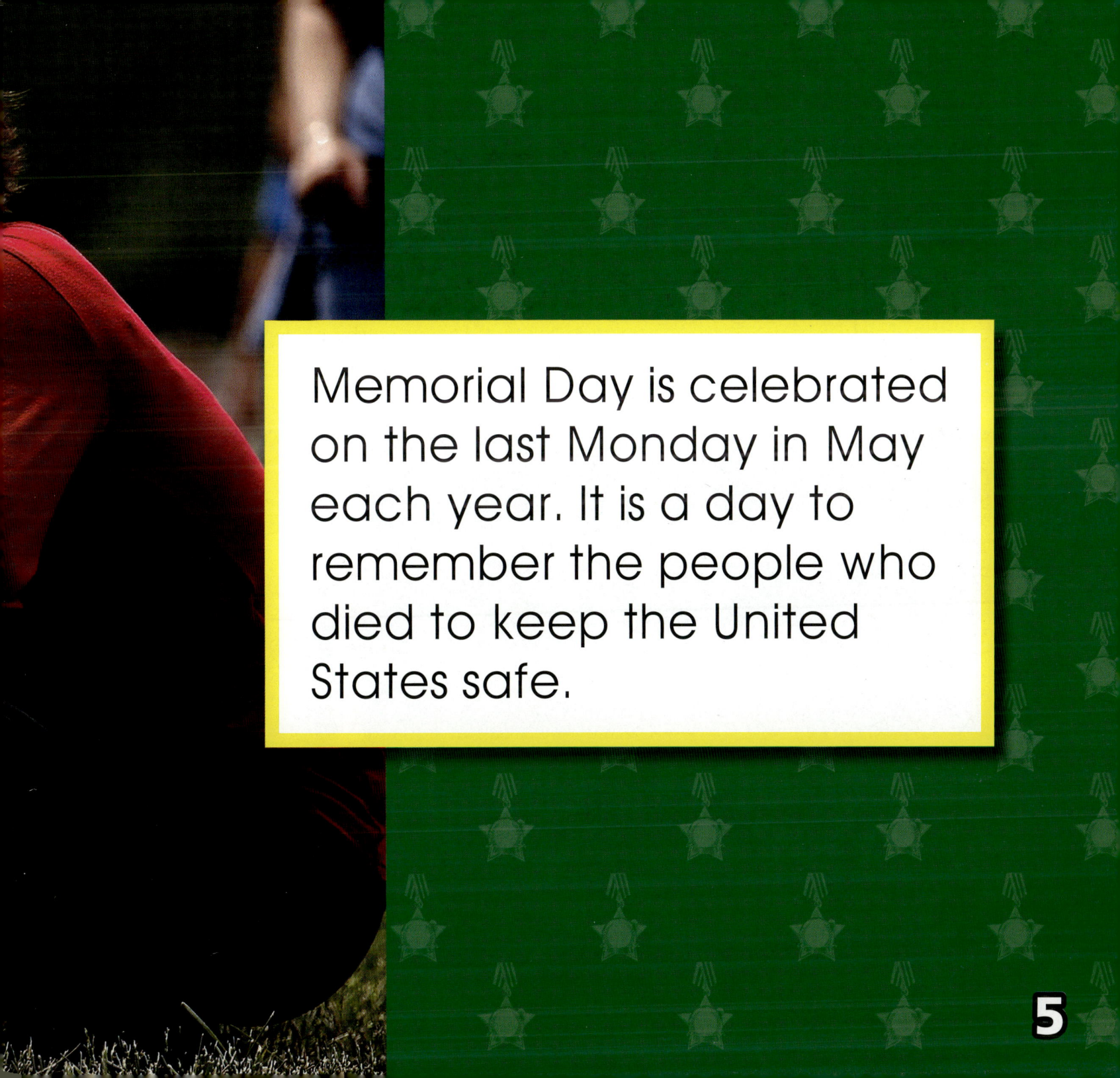

Memorial Day is celebrated on the last Monday in May each year. It is a day to remember the people who died to keep the United States safe.

Memorial Day began near the end of the Civil War. People wanted to honor those who died while fighting.

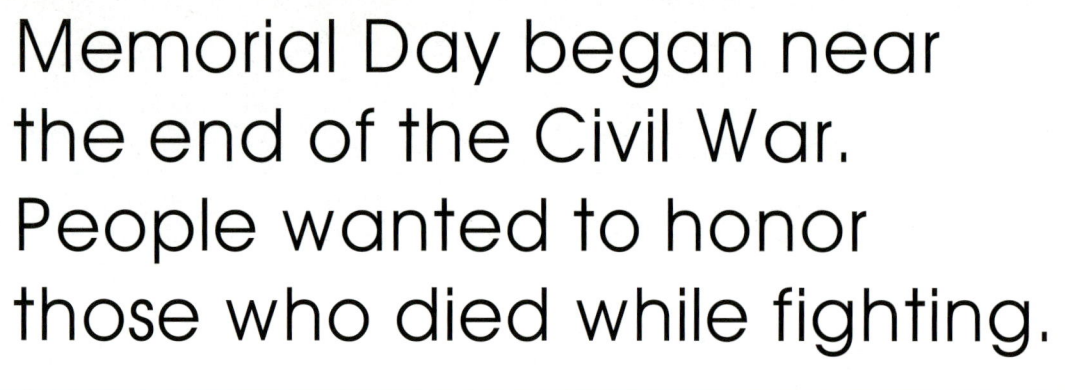

The first official Memorial Day event was held in Waterloo, New York.

John A. Logan was a general in the Civil War. He ordered that May 30th would be a day to remember soldiers who died in the war.

The name "Memorial Day" became official in 1971.

Memorial Day events take place all across the United States. Many cities hold parades and concerts on this day.

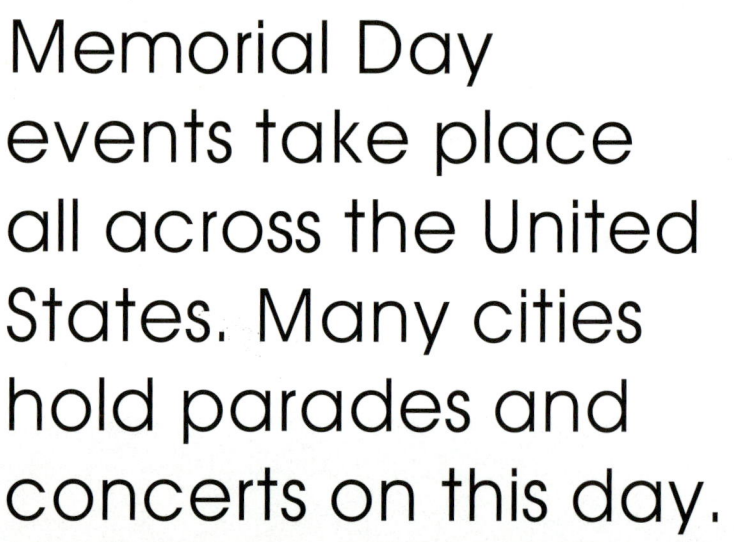

A large concert is held in Washington, D.C. every year.

People gather at monuments and cemeteries to remember fallen soldiers. They lay flowers and wreaths to decorate the soldiers' graves.

Flags are placed in front of the graves at the Arlington National Cemetery for the Memorial Day weekend.

Memorial Day events are held to honor American soldiers. These events stop for one minute of silence at 3:00 pm to remember those who died in battle.

People play a special song called Taps on Memorial Day. It is often heard at military funerals, wreath-laying ceremonies, and memorial services.

Taps is played on an instrument called a bugle.

Memorial Day has many symbols that remind people of the holiday. The Tomb of the Unknowns is a symbol of all soldiers who have died for their country.

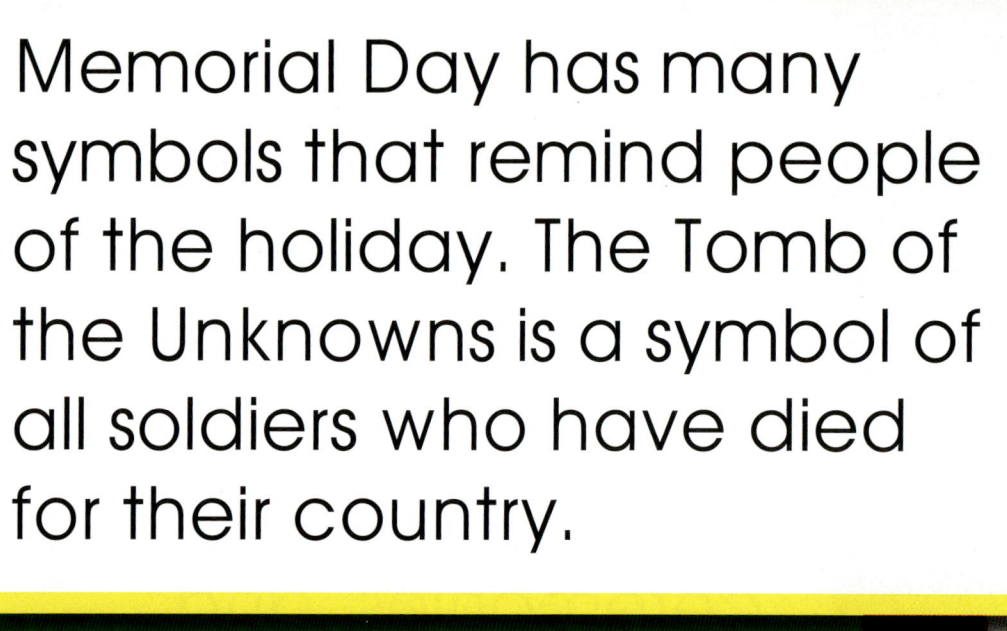

The red poppy is one of the best-known symbols of Memorial Day.

Memorial Day is celebrated in different ways and on different dates in the South. Many southern states have a special day to remember soldiers who fought for the South in the Civil War.

MEMORIAL DAY FACTS

These pages provide more detail about the interesting facts found in the book. They are intended to be used by adults as a learning support to help young readers round out their knowledge of each holiday featured in the *Let's Celebrate American Holidays* series.

Pages 4–5

Memorial Day is celebrated on the last Monday in May each year. This holiday was created to remember the sacrifices made by the men and women who died fighting for the United States during times of war. It was originally known as Decoration Day. The first official Decoration Day ceremony took place on May 30, 1868, at the Arlington National Cemetery in Virginia.

Pages 6–7

Memorial Day began near the end of the Civil War. During the 1800s, the Civil War was the bloodiest war in which the United States had ever fought. When the war ended in 1865, people across the country sought ways to honor the more than 620,000 people who died in the war. Many towns held memorial events. Waterloo, New York, held the first official Memorial Day event on May 5, 1866.

Pages 8–9

John A. Logan was a general in the Civil War. After the war, he helped found an organization of veterans. Logan issued General Order No. 11 on May 5, 1868. It set May 30 as the official day to remember those who died in the Civil War. Over time, the holiday was broadened to include fallen American soldiers from any war. The official name "Memorial Day" was adopted in 1971 and the date was changed from May 30 to the last Monday in May.

Pages 10–11

Memorial Day events take place all across the United States. Memorial Day parades include veterans and current servicemen and servicewomen. A Memorial Day parade has been held in Ironton, Ohio, each year since 1868. More than 1,800 people participate in this parade, and more than 30,000 line the streets to watch. In Washington, D.C., people attend the annual National Memorial Day Concert, and millions more watch the show on television.

Pages 12–13

People gather at monuments and cemeteries to remember fallen soldiers. Formal wreath laying ceremonies are sometimes held, often involving veterans and current soldiers. They lay flowers, flags, and wreaths on the gravestones and monuments in remembrance of those who died fighting. Some ceremonies include prayers and patriotic or military songs.

Pages 14–15

Memorial Day events are held to honor American soldiers. In 2000, Congress passed the National Moment of Remembrance Act. This act set aside 3:00 p.m. local time as a designated moment of silence to remember Americans who fought and died in wars around the world. All across the country, people stop what they are doing and observe one minute of silence.

Pages 16–17

People play a special song called Taps on Memorial Day. There are only 24 notes in Taps. It is a simple, but very moving and powerful song. Taps is thought to have originated from a French bugle signal called "Tattoo." The call was played to notify soldiers when it was time for lights out. It was revised by General Daniel Butterfield during the Civil War and named "Taps" in 1874.

Pages 18–19

Memorial Day has many symbols that remind people of the holiday. The Tomb of the Unknowns at Arlington National Cemetery in Virginia is one of the most iconic symbols. It is the place where three American soldiers from three separate wars have been laid to rest. It is not known who these soldiers are, so they represent all soldiers who fought and died for their country.

Pages 20–21

Memorial Day is celebrated in different ways in the South. Nine southern states celebrate their own days to honor those who died fighting for the Confederacy in the Civil War. Most call this day Confederate Memorial Day, but it is known as Confederate Decoration Day in Tennessee and as Confederate Heroes Day in Texas. The day varies, with dates ranging from April to June.

KEY WORDS

Research has shown that as much as 65 percent of all written material published in English is made up of 300 words. These 300 words cannot be taught using pictures or learned by sounding them out. They must be recognized by sight. This book contains 53 common sight words to help young readers improve their reading fluency and comprehension. This book also teaches young readers several important content words, such as proper nouns. These words are paired with pictures to aid in learning and improve understanding.

Page	Sight Words First Appearance
5	a, day, each, in, is, it, keep, last, on, people, the, to, who, year
6	began, end, first, near, of, those, was, while
9	be, he, name, that, would
10	all, and, every, large, many, place, take, this
13	are, at, for, they
14	American, one, stop, these
17	an, often, play, song
18	country, has, have, their
21	different, ways

Page	Content Words First Appearance
5	May, Memorial Day, Monday, United States
6	Civil War, event, New York, Waterloo
9	general, John A. Logan, soldiers, war
10	cities, concerts, parades, Washington, D.C.
13	Arlington National Cemetery, cemeteries, flags, flowers, graves, monuments, weekend, wreaths
14	battle, minute, silence
17	bugle, ceremonies, funerals, instrument, services, Taps
18	holiday, poppy, symbols, Tomb of the Unknowns
21	Civil War, dates, states, South

Check out www.av2books.com for activities, videos, audio clips, and more!

Go to www.av2books.com.

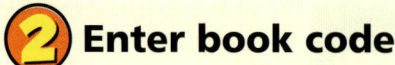
Enter book code. J611318

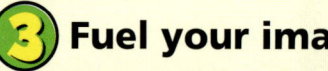
Fuel your imagination online!

www.av2books.com